ON A MISSION

Firefighter

ON A MISSION

Bomb Squad Technician

Border Security

Dogs on Patrol

FBI Agent

Fighter Pilot

Firefighter

Paramedic

Search and Rescue Team

Secret Service Agent

Special Forces

SWAT Team

Undercover Police Officer

ON A MISSION

Firefighter

by K.C. Kelley

Mason Crest
450 Parkway Drive, Suite D
Broomall, PA 19008
www.masoncrest.com

Printed and bound in the United States of America.

Series ISBN: 978-1-4222-3391-7
Hardback ISBN: 978-1-4222-3396-2
EBook ISBN: 978-1-4222-8505-3

First printing
1 3 5 7 9 8 6 4 2

Produced by Shoreline Publishing Group LLC
Santa Barbara, California
Editorial Director: James Buckley Jr.
Designer: Bill Madrid, Production: Sandy Gordon
www.shorelinepublishing.com
Cover image: Mike Eliason, Santa Barbara County Fire Department

Library of Congress Cataloging-in-Publication Data

Kelley, K.C. author.
      Firefighter / by K.C. Kelley.
              pages cm. -- (On a mission!)
     Audience: 12+
     Audience: Grades 7 to 8
     Includes bibliographical references and index.
     ISBN 978-1-4222-3396-2 (hardback) -- ISBN 978-1-4222-3391-7 (series) -- ISBN 978-1-4222-8505-3 (ebook) 1. Fire fighters--Juvenile literature. 2. Fire extinction--Juvenile literature.
I. Title.
HD8039.F5E45 2016
628.9'25--dc23
                       2015009997

Contents

Key Icons to Look For

Words to Understand: These words with their easy-to-understand definitions will increase the reader's understanding of the text, while building vocabulary skills.

Sidebars: This boxed material within the main text allows readers to build knowledge, gain insights, explore possibilities, and broaden their perspectives by weaving together additional information to provide realistic and holistic perspectives.

Research Projects: Readers are pointed toward areas of further inquiry connected to each chapter. Suggestions are provided for projects that encourage deeper research and analysis.

Text-Dependent Questions: These questions send the reader back to the text for more careful attention to the evidence presented here.

Series Glossary of Key Terms: This back-of-the-book glossary contains terminology used throughout this series. Words found here increase the reader's ability to read and comprehend higher-level books and articles in this field.

Emergency!

Fires at night present additional challenges for firefighters. At the fire in this story, they even battled a live electrical wire.

The really bad ones always seem to come at night. Santa Barbara, California, city firefighters were resting in their fire stations when the calls started to come in. "Major structure fire . . . all engines report." This was going to be a big one.

A fire had started at an apartment building in a crowded area of downtown Santa Barbara. If firefighters didn't act soon, it could spread quickly.

As they reached the scene of the fire, the commanders quickly looked over the situation. It's a massive job to tackle a fire of this size. Taking it on takes teamwork, planning, the right equipment, and the hard work of the boots on the ground. Several engines and trucks pulled into position. Firefighters scrambled off their vehicles to start pulling hoses and hooking them up to hydrants.

To make matters worse, the weather was getting in their way, even for normally calm and pleasant Santa Barbara.

"It was one of those humid nights that kept the smoke down low to the ground so that they could not even see where the fire was," a fire captain told reporters after the incident was over.

Words to Understand

backcountry a wide area of open land behind a range of mountains

hot lap a firefighting term that means walking all the way around a burning structure to locate the best place to direct water at flames

One fire engine's captain did a **"hot lap,"** which means walking around a structure to find the best place from which to attack the fire.

When firefighters got the input from the captain's hot lap, they reached the buildings on fire and quickly searched for possible victims. Human beings are more important than buildings, so the firefighters made sure that everyone had gotten out.

With the residents all accounted for, the crews started to pour water on the fire, which had leaped into a nearby parking lot to attack vehicles, too. Advancing behind the massive power of the hoses, the teams found fire wherever they went. The darkness added a menacing air to the flames, as they danced and glowed about. Ashes and sparks flew like snow amid the mist and smoke.

The flames lit up another potential disaster—a neighboring property is a historic building, while on the other side stands an apartment house with 16 units.

"There was the apartment building on fire," a fire captain told local media. "Another, smaller building next door was completely consumed by the fire. And there was also an old Victorian building that was part of the Flying A Studios. We wanted to try to keep the fire from spreading there, too."

While one firefighter pulls away burning material, another attacks the flames with the hose.

Using their knowledge of the science of flame, firefighters often crawl through a scene to stay below dangerous smoke and other gases.

Until the end of World War I, Santa Barbara's Flying A Studios was one of the busiest film production companies in the United States. Specializing in Westerns and often using the local **backcountry** for shooting, Flying A helped jump-start an industry that has come to symbolize southern California. The building was a living reminder of those important days in local history.

Protecting people's lives is the main responsibility of any first responder. Taking care of valuable and important buildings does have a place on the list, however. If firefighters could knock down this fire quickly, they would save a piece of history. They knew that the residents were all safe, so it was time to protect property.

However, as in any fire situation, things can change in an instant. As the firefighters continued to find new pockets of flame, another danger appeared suddenly. From high above them, burned by the massive fire, a live power line landed in a blaze of sparks. Stepping on that electrical wire would mean instant death.

An already touchy situation for Santa Barbara firefighters just got a lot more dangerous.

Later, in the "Mission Accomplished" chapter, find out how the firefighters successfully completed their mission. First, learn more about how firefighters do their jobs and the gear they use.

Millions of kids dream of becoming a firefighter. Only the bravest and hardest-working people make that dream come true, however.

Chapter 1

Mission Prep

"When I grow up, I want to be a firefighter!" Young people have declared that as a goal for decades. The image of the brave firefighter risking life and limb to pull people out of burning buildings is legendary. Fire is one of the things that most people fear. Firefighters are the people who face that fear and save the day.

Communities have had to rely on firefighters for thousands of years, of course. From the first "bucket brigades" to today's high-tech flame-fighting crews, the job has called for the bravest people around. Firefighters go wherever the mission takes them, from high-rise fires to burning apartments, from vehicle rescue to flames scorching the forest. The goal of helping people remains at the top, but getting there takes a lot of training and, today, involves the use of high-tech gear.

Firefighting History

Firefighters have been needed since people started living in cities and buildings. Ancient civilizations relied on buckets of water or dirt to smother fires. Rome had groups of citizens more than 2,000 years ago who

Words to Understand

justify explain using reasons or math in order to prove a point

rig another name for a fire-fighting vehicle

Antique firefighting gear often can be found in museums, such as this British fire helmet from the 1800s.

called the alarm in case of fire. There was no department—everyone helped put out the fire.

Citizen firefighters were the norm for centuries. There were no professional, full-time firefighters. Sometimes an army might be called out to help at a major event, but they were not trained to fight fires. An example of early American firefighting came in 1648, when the colony of New York paid men to walk the streets at night with rattles, ready to alert people to a fire.

During all that time, people had little more than buckets to throw water and axes to pull burning material apart to prevent a fire from spreading. Most firefighting was just to prevent it from spreading, not to put it out. The idea of rescuing people was more luck than any sort of skill. In fact, even fire hoses were not part of firefighting gear until the 1600s; even then, pumps to bring water to the hoses were operated by hand. The streams were not very powerful. The city of Paris, France, was one of the first to pay for those rolling pumps to be made available throughout the city. The city had a fire brigade of volunteers by the early 1700s.

The key development in how cities fought fires came with plumbing systems. As water began to be piped around cities to feed sinks and toilets, firefighters gained better access to water. In the early 1800s, the first fire hydrants were installed in Philadelphia, and the idea spread quickly. It was not the answer to every fire—hydrants were not located everywhere for decades—but it was a huge first step.

In cities or areas without such devices, firefighters relied on horse-drawn pumps. Buckets were used to fill a large container on a wagon. Using muscle power at first and, later, steam power, the water was pulled from the container through the hose and directed at the flames. By the 1800s, the new steam engines greatly improved how firefighters battled fires. Drawn by horses, the steam-powered pumps sped to the site of the fire, and the men got to work.

In the early 1900s, the development of motor vehicles gave firefighters another improvement. Now their fire vehicles could get to fires faster, powered by gas engines. The pumps, too, worked better with engine power. Stronger and more powerful jets of water were possible.

Advances in firefighting have come rapidly in the past decades. The gear has continued to improve, making firefighters safer and helping them deal with emergencies faster than ever.

Fire Departments

Until the mid-1800s, the ways in which fire departments were organized varied from city to city. Some were all-volunteer units (Benjamin Franklin organized one in Philadelphia in 1736!), others were paid by groups of local business owners who wanted protection for their buildings. That sometimes resulted in firefighters working to save only the buildings they were paid to protect, while others nearby burned. That led to races between competing companies, too. Arguments would break out over who got to a fire first—and who should be paid to do the work. Fire engines worked to have the fastest horses and best drivers, along with the bravest men to put out the fire.

In 1853, the city of Cincinnati, home to the first working fire engine powered by steam, created the first professional, city-run department. As cities became larger and larger, and more and more people lived in crowded buildings, fires became an even larger danger. Cities recognized that and began forming similar departments. The men who worked in them were trained on the equipment of the time and organized so that areas of the city were always covered. The heroic nature of the firefighter as a separate person, not just

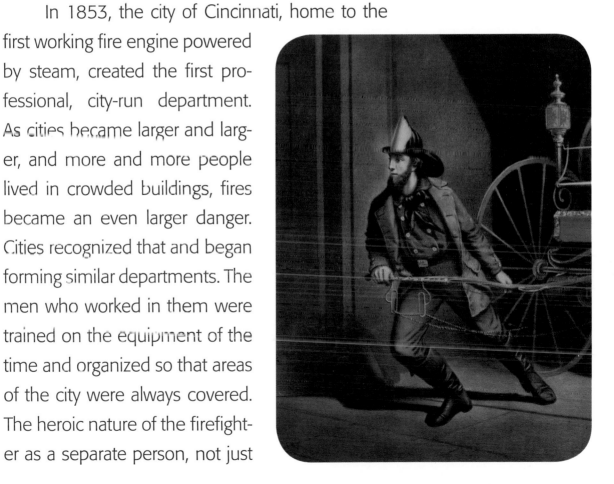

Painted by Louis Maurer and printed by Currier and Ives in 1858, this image shows a typical American firefighter of the period.

Getting Organized

More than 1.2 million firefighters serve the United States each year. About 70 percent of them are volunteers, while the rest are full-time professionals. Most of the pros work in large cities. In smaller towns and rural areas, volunteer firefighters still play an important role. Often, these areas do not have enough people to support a large, full-time professional department. Their services might not be needed enough to justify the expense. However, protection is still needed. Volunteer departments fill the bill. Citizens undergo limited training and sometimes work with a small staff of professionals. A person might even end up being called to his own neighborhood to deal with an emergency.

In a large city, a fire department is organized into fire stations. Each station covers a part of the city, though several stations might come together to deal with a large fire.

a volunteer from the community, began to arise. Departments created uniforms so that their men stood out. Earning a job called for strength and toughness. Most did not pay well, so the honor of serving was part of the appeal. Over the decades, more and more cities moved to professional and trained departments.

Life as a Firefighter

A career as a firefighter can be dangerous, of course, but it also is rewarding. The first step is to have the motivation. A person has to want to take on the challenge, which is both a physical and a mental one. It's physical because of the need to carry heavy loads, work while wearing lots of gear, and being able to work in hot and wet conditions no matter what. It's a mental challenge because firefighters have to overcome their fear.

They also must have the ability to bounce back after experiencing tragedy. Not every fire rescue is successful, and firefighters have to learn to deal with grief about such incidents and still get back to work and keep trying.

It can be dangerous work, of course. In 2014, 106 firefighters died and nearly 30,000 were injured. Similar numbers were reported for other recent years.

The desire to help, and to give back to a community, drives most people into the fire services around the world. People drawn to firefighting also like the idea of working with their hands and having an active job instead of one that is mostly sitting around an office. Firefighters have to remain in top physical shape. They also continue to learn new techniques as they progress in their careers.

Most departments have several levels of firefighting roles. The basic unit is the fire company, which is three to six people who work together on a particular **rig**, or fire vehicle. For example, a three-person team on a pumper includes a cap-

The engineer uses the instrument panel on the engine to direct the flow of water to hoses as needed by firefighters.

tain, a firefighter, and a fire engineer. The captain is in charge of the crew. He directs the work of the team, as well as takes part in fighting the fire. The firefighter handles most of the gear and helps with rescue work. The engineer safely drives the rig and focuses on the vehicle, making sure that it works properly. The engineer is responsible for pumping the water through the hoses to the firefighters at the nozzle. That makes it certain to get the "wet stuff on the hot stuff," as the firefighters say.

Fire companies are gathered into larger units such as fire stations, which might include several companies. Each station has a captain or chief who supervises all the companies. Larger departments also have leaders at several levels, including battalion chiefs or division chiefs. They all work under the department's top fire chief, who oversees the city-wide work, including hiring new firefighters and preparing a budget with city or county officials.

One type of fire professional that many people see is the public information officer (PIO). The news media wants to tell the story of most major fires or emergencies. It gets its information from the PIO, who often appears on camera. Before the PIOs have stories to tell, though, firefighters have to learn the lessons that will keep alive the people they help.

Text-Dependent Questions

1. What did early American colonists use to alert people to fires?
2. In what city was the first professional department in the United States located?
3. What is the role of the PIO?

Research Project

What is the history of your area's fire department? Go on its Web site or visit a fire station and find out when your city, county, or area first got a professional fire service. How many people are working in it now? How many vehicles and stations does the department have?

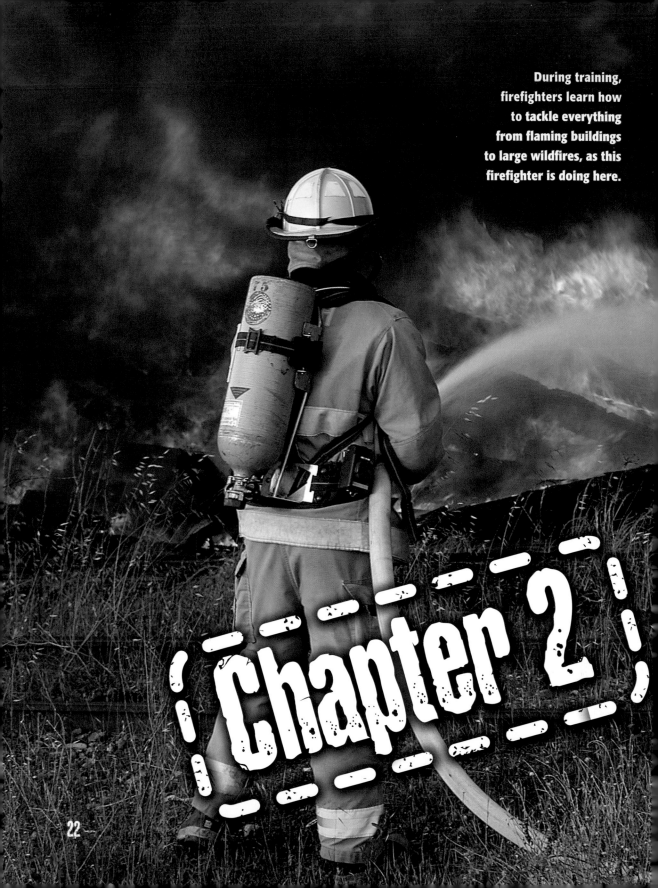

During training, firefighters learn how to tackle everything from flaming buildings to large wildfires, as this firefighter is doing here.

Chapter 2

Training Mind and Body

Decked out in fire helmet, protective coat, and heavy rubber boots, the firefighter aims the hose at the flames. With a mighty rush, the water powers out of the end of the nozzle. As the water hits the flames, there is a huge cloud of smoke and steam. The fire scene is noisy and chaotic, but the firefighter loves it. This firefighter got to the fire scene on a speeding truck, but every firefighter has to go through a long process to earn the right to do the job.

The process can take years, but for people who really want to make firefighting their life's work, it's worth the wait. Most people applying to become firefighters understand what this statement from the Hayward,

California, Fire Department means: "Becoming a firefighter is truly a 'calling' that should not be taken lightly. It is one of the most demanding, but rewarding professions [in the world]. Firefighters are a band of brothers and sisters who risk their lives daily to protect the citizens of their communities."

That sense of mission is part of every firefighter's life. That mission starts in school.

At the Academy

Firefighters first have to earn a high school diploma. College is not necessary to apply, though many firefighters do earn a college degree. Some, in fact, take firefighting classes at community colleges before applying to the fire departments. The higher up people move in the fire service, the more education they'll need. Chiefs and department heads often earn master's degrees in several fields.

Along with a high school diploma, a person aiming to be a firefighter should make sure to be very fit. In fact, most departments call for a very difficult fitness test even before a person's application will be accepted. Applicants might also be asked to take a test to find out more about their general mental abilities.

Jobs as professional firefighters are very popular. Thousands of people apply for each spot that opens up. Some people have to apply many times to several departments before they are accepted into the training programs.

Of course, just making it into that program is no guarantee that a person will end up with the job. Fire academies take future firefighters on an intense journey that can last several months of full-time work. Classroom lessons cover the science of fire, fire department rules, and emergency medicine. Work in the field includes learning to use hoses, ladders, and other fire gear. Overall, firefighter trainees will spend more than 600 hours in class and in the field, along with many more hours studying on their own.

Teamwork first: Even raising and climbing a ladder calls for firefighters to work together.

Women in Firefighting

Today, women can join in just about any part of professional firefighting. They make up only about three to four percent of full-time firefighters, however. Though that means only about 11,000 of the 300,000-plus firefighters are women, that's more than there were in earlier days. Only a handful of women took part in the volunteer fire brigades in the 1800s. Several others were part of rural volunteer groups in the 1900s.

It was not until 1974 that a woman earned a full-time job as a professional firefighter. The barriers used to be the reputation of the fire service as a "boys' club." Today, the only real barriers are physical. Women have to be able to do all the work that men can do. If a woman has the strength and the will, she can do the job.

Some of the training exercises might include learning to put on their gear quickly and efficiently. When racing to get to a fire, every second counts. Firefighters pride themselves in being able to gear up and go in seconds. That takes time to learn, however.

Trainees also learn how to carry victims safely. The last thing you want to do is drop them or injure yourself while trying to help. There are right ways and wrong ways to transport an injured person.

Trainees who think they know how to climb a ladder quickly learn that there's a wrong way, and then there is the firefighter way. **Ascending** a ladder while carrying firefighting gear and wearing heavy boots takes a series of careful steps. Firefighters, though, have to make those steps quickly as they race up to help.

Putting Out Fires

Classroom work can only take a firefighter so far. To prepare future firefighters, there is nothing like the real thing. After learning how to use the hoses, ladders, and protective gear, trainees face the fire itself. Some departments have a permanent fire tower that can be lit over and over again. Working with their instructors, trainees do the work needed to extinguish the fire. Other academies might obtain a building scheduled for demolition and light it on fire. The controlled burn accomplishes two things: It gets rid of an unwanted building, and it gives trainees hands-on experience fighting a live fire.

The key to fighting fires safely is communication and teamwork. They are the most important lessons that trainees learn. It's not just one firefighter aiming a hose, it's a group of firefighters working together to get that heavy hose in place, hold it steady, and provide the water. Trainees take turns doing each of the jobs on a hose crew so they will be ready to pitch in wherever needed.

The weight and spraying power of the fire hose means that a group of firefighters has to work together to carry, aim, and spray.

As trainees learn the techniques to fight fire, they also learn about fire itself. Fire is a part of nature, and it behaves in predictable ways, most of the time. Hot air always rises, for example, so the path of most fires is upward. By knocking down the base, or bottom, of a fire, firefighters can shut down its power. Since the smoke will rise to the ceiling, that also is why firefighters are taught to crawl through a smoke-filled area. Firefighters also learn how fire moves through a structure, what paths it takes from room to room, and how it can "hide" in walls without being seen.

Fire needs air to burn, so firefighters have to avoid providing air to a fire. Opening a window or a door in a burning room can cause the fire to spread very suddenly, so firefighters have to use caution when doing that. On other occasions, making a hole in a roof to "vent" a fire does provide air, but it also lets the fire, smoke, and hot gasses get out instead of just spread inside to burn more of the attic. It also helps clear the air so the firefighters working below will be able to see better.

Other Emergencies

Fires are actually not the most common emergencies firefighters face. As first responders, they are called to the scene of many different events, from car crashes to building collapses to medical emergencies. Their training covers what to do to in all these situations. For most departments, 75 percent of the calls firefighters go on are medical emergencies.

At a car wreck, the first move is to secure the scene and make sure that the car's gasoline will not ignite. If there is already a fire, firefighters use water or foam to put it out quickly. The next move is to assess the victims. Can they walk on their own? If so, firefighters guide them to a safe place.

Thanks to the brave work of firefighters, everyone in this horribly smashed car made it out of the wreck alive.

Often, however, victims are trapped in the cars. Fire crews are trained to take apart vehicles safely while protecting the victims. They use their emergency medicine knowledge to stabilize the patient until paramedics arrive. Tearing apart the car, meanwhile, can call for a bit of creativity and some powerful tools. The most frequently used tool is the "jaws of life," a handheld device that pulls apart metal or opens stuck doors.

At the scene of a medical emergency, firefighters with paramedic training can start treating the patient right away. The other firefighters assist by clearing the scene for the ambulance or protecting the victim from the environment.

A hazardous material, or "**hazmat**," chemical spill is another emergency firefighters face. The government has identified 84,000 types of hazardous chemicals that travel America's roads and rails. At any time, they may spill accidentally. Wearing special protective gear, firefighters clean up or **neutralize** the spilled materials. Firefighters might help get people out of a collapsed building, protect an area from a downed power line, or rescue someone stuck in a tree. When the radio crackles with news of a new emergency, firefighters quickly learn that they never know where they might end up next.

Fighting Wildfires

Departments whose responsibility includes fields, forests, meadows, and other outdoor areas must deal with wildfires. Putting out a huge fire that covers thousands of acres demands specialized skills.

In a wildfire, flames can leap up and over firefighters. **Embers** can be carried by wind more than a mile and land around and behind the crews, creating new dangers. The wind can change direction suddenly, pushing a wall of fire toward firefighters. Wildfires can move as quickly as a car racing down the highway!

The best way to deal with wildfires is by cutting off the fuel. Commanders position their men around the edges of a large fire. Crews use bulldozers, hand tools, and hoses to create a wide firebreak. By removing the vegetation that can burn, the fire will go out once it reaches the cleared area. Dropping water or chemicals on the fire from helicopters or airplanes also can help contain it.

The work of becoming a firefighter is hard and takes time. In the end, everyone who goes through it is gratified when those lessons come into play in the field. When firefighters save a life thanks to what they learned at the academy, they knows that every lesson counts.

Text-Dependent Questions

1. Where do most firefighting trainees learn their trade?
2. Name two non-fire emergencies firefighters might have to deal with.
3. What is the key way that firefighters try to stop wildfires?

Research Project

Do you have what it takes? Look up the firefighters' fitness test for your local department. What are some of the tasks they have to do? How close can you come to the marks they set for running, sit-ups, push-ups, etc.?

Chapter 3

The reflective strips on the turnout gear help identify firefighters in any condition. A radio at the collar helps them stay in contact.

Tools and Technology

Firefighters head into any emergency with their personal bravery, the skills and techniques they have learned, and a team of experts around them. They also bring a host of tools and technology that has made firefighting today safer and more effective than ever.

Turnout Gear

The familiar protective clothing worn by firefighters is known as "turnout gear." It's the outfit they wear when they turn out for a fire or emergency. Over pants made of flame-resistant cloth and T-shirts, often decorated with department logos, go heavy pants and a heavy jacket. They are made of three layers of protection. The innermost **thermal** liner helps deflect the heat of a fire they might face. The next layer is a moisture barrier. It helps prevent water, chemicals, or vapors from reaching the firefighter's skin. The outer shell is made of a tough fabric that resists tears, protects against sharp or rough surfaces, and adds another layer of thermal protection. It can be dark or very dim in a fire scene, so the

Words to Understand

arson a fire that was started deliberately; arson is a crime
thermal having to do with heat or flames

With helmet strapped in place over a face mask for oxygen, a firefighter practices climbing amid the smoke.

shell also has numerous strips of reflective cloth. The strips help firefighters pick their teammates out of the darkness. Turnout gear is sometimes called "bunker gear," after the bunks where old-time volunteers kept their working clothes when they were asleep.

On their feet, firefighters wear rubber boots. They are made of very thick, water-repelling rubber over harder shells. In the soles and toes of most models, steel plates help protect the feet from falling objects or from stepping on sharp things.

The fire helmet has been the same basic shape since the 1800s. The wide brim and long back protect the head and neck from falling debris. The high, heavy crown helps when crawling or climbing by keeping the head from whacking into walls or buildings. Attached to some helmets today is a thick plastic face shield for eye protection. A chinstrap keeps the helmet from falling off, while the badge on the front identifies the department and rank.

To breathe in the smoke filled air, firefighters wear a bottle filled with compressed air on their back. They wear a mask over their face to safely breathe good air in all the smoke. Depending upon the firefighters and how hard they are working, the bottle can last as much as 15 minutes or as little as seven minutes. An alarm sounds to let them know when they are getting low on air. They must then return to change out the bottle with a full one.

Firefighters also have a small device attached to the air-pack harness. The device emits a sharp beeping sound if the firefighter stops moving. That helps firefighters keep track of each other in the dark and the chaos of a fire scene. In case a firefighter is trapped and cannot respond, the beeps lead his teammates to him.

By spinning this nozzle at the end of the fire hose, firefighters can control the shape of the spray and the amount of water flow.

Hoses and Nozzles

Fire hoses have retained their basic shape and size for many years, though the materials they are made of have been modernized. Early hoses were all leather and leaked badly. With the invention of rubber, hoses became much more dependable and flexible. The newer fire hoses were made with rubber interior tubes and covered with fabric. As the tubes filled with water, the fabric could stretch and expand to hold the hose's shape.

Today, fire hoses are still made with rubber and fabric, although both those materials are now made from heat-resistant and durable compounds. They are also created to be lighter and easier to maneuver. While most garden hoses retain their tubular shape, fire hoses can be flattened when not filled with water. That makes it easier to roll up the hose or to store it flat in the back of a truck. Firefighters spend much more time cleaning, rolling, and storing their hoses than they do aiming them at fires. That time spent caring for their hoses, however, often can be a lifesaver.

At the end of the hose is a nozzle that can project the water in many different ways. The firefighters at the end adjust the nozzle to produce whatever spread is needed. Some fires call for a full-blast stream. Others are fought with a heavy misting spray, while still others are best attacked with a wide flow.

At some fires, water is not the answer. At airports, for instance, a special foam is used to cover jet fuel flames or spilled fuel. The foam robs the flames of oxygen and helps them go out.

Vehicles

Getting to the scene of the fire is often the loudest and most exciting part of an emergency. Firefighters pull on

Hand Tools

Sometimes, firefighters need to break through a wall or door to reach the fire or a victim. For this, they often use a fire axe. The axe also can be used to pull down burning materials to expose fires to the stream of a hose. Firefighters might also strike down a wall or ceiling that might otherwise fall on someone. Wrenches are carried to help turn off a water or gas supply. Hammers or sledges might be used for some of the same roles as the axe.

One of the coolest handheld devices now in use is a heat seeker, or thermal-imaging camera. By looking at the screen of this device, firefighters can "see" hidden fire or heat behind or through walls. They can locate fire they can't otherwise see, which helps them put it out more quickly, and also prevents them from going into a dangerous situation unprepared.

their gear and climb aboard an engine, a truck, or a hook-and-ladder. As the siren screams and cars get out of the way, the fire vehicle races at high speed through busy streets. The vehicle used depends on the type of emergency.

Fire engines are the larger vehicles and earn their name engine because they can pump water onto a fire from a tank within. They carry many ladders and other fire gear. The water can come out through hoses or from a nozzle mounted to the top.

Fire trucks do not carry water, but they do carry hoses and other gear firefighters need. Trucks bring emergency medical gear, axes or shovels, and hoses and nozzles that can be attached to a hydrant or to a pumper engine. The hook-and-ladder trucks are the longer versions, with an additional driver at the back to steer the extra-long engine around corners. The long ladder atop such vehicles is sometimes called the snorkel. It can be raised to reach very high in a burning building.

Specialty fire vehicles include rugged pickup trucks used in brushfires; command post trucks that include maps and communications gear; and hazmat trucks for dealing with chemical spills.

From the helmets on their heads to the boots on their feet, firefighters are equipped to handle any emergency. As much as they love their gear, however, firefighters know that their most important tools are training and teamwork.

Text-Dependent Questions

1. What's the difference between a fire truck and a fire engine?
2. What do airport fire departments use instead of water?
3. How can thermal-imaging cameras help firefighters?

Research Project

Do you have a fire extinguisher in your home? If you do, check the date. Is it still good? If you don't, ask your parents to buy one or several for your home. Read online or talk to a fire department about the best places to keep a fire extinguisher (kitchen, garage, etc.). Some departments even offer extinguisher training.

Chapter 4

No matter how high the flames stretch into th
sky, firefighters know that attacking the bas
of the flames will have the best resul

Mission Accomplished!

Within a few moments of getting the late-night call to an apartment fire, all seven engines from the Santa Barbara City Fire Department are on the scene. The flashing lights make the night sky glow red, white, and orange. Firefighter flashlights dance through the dark, making sure all the apartments are empty.

The battle against the flames calls for all the firefighters' expertise. They run hose after hose onto the property. At least two buildings are on fire already, with more, including a nearby historic structure, at risk.

To make matters worse, the fire has burned through a live electrical wire, which sparks across the path the firefighters would have to take toward some of the fire.

"They could see the wire popping even as they were trying to get water to the building on fire," a fire captain told reporters. "Even above them, there were other power lines.

Words to Understand

exposure the area on buildings that is in danger of catching fire, but has not yet been affected

"We have to be aware of everything around us when we're working on a structure fire. We can't just look at the flames, there are other dangers and issues to deal with."

The teamwork training that started at the academies comes into play once again. While some firefighters work to shut off the power, others advance toward the burning buildings. Engineers work feverishly on the pumpers to make sure the hose teams have the water pressure they need. Captains and commanders set up maps and gather information that will help them direct their teams to the right places.

Slowly but surely, the firefighters gain on the fire. The major flames are dampened, and some of the danger to neighboring buildings eases. There is no time to rest, though. With one building on its way to being a total loss, the crews try to make sure the blaze is out for good. It can take only a short while to knock down large flames. It can take hours to track down lingering hot spots or burning material.

While some crews focus on mopping up, other fire crews are put in place to guard neighboring structures for **exposure**. The sides of nearby buildings are wet down, and brush is cleared away from their sides. A flying ember or spark will have a tougher time causing trouble to a wet building or to a dirt-covered place.

This action from another nighttime fire shows the fierceness of the flames, even as firefighters race toward them, hoses at the ready.

"We're fortunate that we made a pretty good stop here and kept the fire from jumping," the captain concluded.

The firefighters still have hours of work ahead of them, putting away gear, helping clean up the fire scene of debris, and making sure residents have a safe place to go. For some of the firefighters, this is the beginning of another long shift. For some, it's finally time to go home.

Find Out More

Books

Cooper, Michael L. *Fighting Fire! Ten of the Deadliest Fires in American History and How We Fought Them.* New York: Henry Holt, 2014.

Dombrowski, Bob. *38 Years: A Detroit Firefighter's Story.* New York: Page Publishing, 2013.

Klinoff, Robert W. *Introduction to Fire Protection.* Boston: Cengage Learning, 2011. Note: This large, textbook-like product features everything an introductory firefighter might need to know.

Web Sites

www.hulu.com/on-duty
Watch episodes of *On Duty*, a reality show featuring tales from the Santa Barbara City firefighters.

www.fireengineering.com
A magazine site with articles on all aspects of firefighting life.

www.firescience.org
A site that includes lots of information about becoming a firefighter.

Series Glossary of Key Terms

apprehending capturing and arresting someone who has committed a crime

assassinate kill somebody, especially a political figure

assessment the act of gathering information and making a decision about a particular topic

contraband material that is illegal to possess

cryptography another word for writing in code

deployed put to use, usually in a military or law-enforcement operation

dispatcher a person who announces emergencies over police radio and helps organize the efforts of first responders

elite among the very best; part of a select group of successful experts

evacuated moved to a safe location, away from danger

federal related to the government of the United States, as opposed to the government of an individual state or city

forensic having to do with crime scene evidence

instinctive based on natural impulse and done without instruction

interrogate to question a person as part of an official investigation

Kevlar an extra-tough fabric used in bulletproof vests

search-and-rescue the work of finding survivors after a disaster occurs, or the team that does this work

stabilize make steady or secure; also, in medicine, make a person safe to transport

surveillance the act of watching another person or a place, usually from a hidden location

trauma any physical injury to the body, usually involving bleeding

visa travel permit issued by a government to a citizen for a specific trip

warrant official document that allows the police to do something, such as arrest a person

Index

Photo Credits

Mike Eliason, Santa Barbara County Fire Department: 6, 9, 10, 20, 25, 30, 45.

Dreamstime.com: Susan Sheldon 12; Peterphoto7 22; Ververidis 28; Frenzel 34; Potowizard 36; Twigra 37; Jay-s 42.

Chris McKenna: 14. Painted by Louis Maurer: 17

About the Author

K.C. Kelley is the California-based author of more than 100 nonfiction books for young readers on a wide variety of topics. The author thanks Mike Eliason, public information officer for the Santa Barbara County Fire Department and an award-winning photographer, for his assistance with this book.